E. B. O'Callaghan

A Brief and True Narrative of the Hostile Conduct of the Barbarous Natives

Towards the Dutch Nation

E. B. O'Callaghan

A Brief and True Narrative of the Hostile Conduct of the Barbarous Natives
Towards the Dutch Nation

ISBN/EAN: 9783337054182

Printed in Europe, USA, Canada, Australia, Japan

Cover: Foto ©ninafisch / pixelio.de

More available books at **www.hansebooks.com**

A

BRIEF AND TRUE

NARRATIVE

OF THE

HOSTILE CONDUCT

OF THE

BARBAROUS NATIVES

TOWARDS

The Dutch Nation.

TRANSLATED BY

E. B. O'CALLAGHAN.

ALBANY:

J. MUNSELL, 78 STATE STREET.

MDCCCLXIII.

To the Reader.

THE Paper, of which the following is a Tranſlation, is to be found in Vol. VI of the Original Dutch MSS. in the Secretary's Office, Albany, N. Y. It conſiſts of a Petition dated 31ſt October, 1655, one copy of which was addreſſed to the States General of the United Netherlands ; another to the Burgomaſ-ters and Common Council of the City of Am-ſterdam, and a third to the Directors of the Weſt India Company, Chamber at Amſterdam. In order to throw further light on the ſubject, a few illuſtrative Documents are added in the Appendix.

NARRATIVE.

WE Your High Mighti-nesses and Honours Pe-tioners, with due Reverence and in all Humility, and so far as our Knowledge extends, with all Justice and Truth, repre-sent --- That through God's Providence and under Your Commission and Protection, and with the Knowledge and Consent of the Lord Directors, we have transported ourselves and settled down in this Pro-

vince of *New Netherland*,---a
Country not varying from our
Fatherland in refpect of Climate and Fertility---in which,
too, we Your Petitioners and
Subjects can eafily earn a Live-
lihood; have for a long time
fupported ourfelves and could
indeed ftill further live with
apparent Hope of producing
there many and divers good
Crops and Commodities, if
we could be in any wife fe-
cured, and remain protected
from the Moleftations, Vexa-
tions and Murders of the Native
Barbarians, at whofe Hands we
have fuffered many Infolencies,
in the Slaying of our Cattle

New Nether-
land like Fa-
therland in
Climate, &c.

Hoftilities of
the Natives
towards the
Dutch.

and Killing of our People, with
the Particulars whereof, in paft
Times, we will not incumber
Your Honours.

In order not to fpin out a
too tedious Relation nor divert
Your Attention from graver
and weightier Affairs, we will
only fay, in a word, that after
a two years' War had been
waged againft the *Dutch* by
divers barbarous *Indian* Tribes,
the Lawfulnefs or Unlawfulnefs
whereof we will not difcufs to
any one's Difparagement, a
firm and irrefragable Peace was
finally concluded, in the Year
*Sixteen Hundred Five and
Forty*, with the Natives afore-

Peace conclud-
ed in 1645.

Conditions
thereof.

said, on the Conditions hereunto annexed.

Since then In-
dians kill many
Cattle and mur-
der several Per-
fons.

Those Indian Nations have,
since that time, without any
cause as far as we know, not
only slain and killed many
Animals, such as Cows, Horses
and Hogs, your Subjects' property, but even cruelly murdered ten Persons, *videlicet:*
First, *Symon Walingen* in the
second Year after the Peace
had been concluded ; the Wife
of *Jan Pieterfen* on *Long Ifland* in the year *Sixteen Hundred One and Fifty;* in the
Year *Sixteen Hundred and
Fifty-two,* four Persons on this
Island of *Manhattan;* again,

one Year after that, three People on *Staten Ifland*, and laft
Year *Jochim Pieterfen Kuyter*
in his own Houfe.

The Supreme Government
of this Province hath demanded
the Murderers, but thefe have
always been refufed; certes,
have never been forthcoming;
and for the fake of Peace and
out of confideration for the
good and advantage of the
Country and its People, the
Government hath without any
Manifeftation of Hoftility or
Revenge, winked at this Infraction of the Peace.

The Murderers demanded, but not given up.

Infraction of the Peace winked at.

Now, it hath further come
to pafs, that on the *fifteenth* of

Director General goes to reduce the Swedes at the South River.

the laſt month, *September*--- after the *Honourable* the Director General had, purſuant to Your Honours' Orders and Deſpatches, taken his Departure, with the few Soldiers belonging to this Province, for the *South River* of *New Netherland*, for the purpoſe of reſenting the Affronts and Inſults ſuffered from the *Swedes*, and of reducing that River again under this Province--- (the Bleſſing of God on which

A large body of Savages land at New Amſterdam.

Expedition we moſt gratefully acknowledge)---*fourteen* Days after the *Honble* Director's Departure, very early in the Morning, nigh this City of

New Amfterdam, arrived *fixty-four* Canoes full of *Indians,* who before fcarcely anyone was yet rifen fcattered them-felves throughout this City, and during the following Day, in many Houfes and to divers Burghers offered numerous In-fults, all which to particularize would draw this humble Peti-tion to too great a length.

Their infolent behaviour.

Thereupon their *Sackimas,* or Chiefs, being fummoned be-fore the Council, gave very fair Words, and promifed to depart before the Evening. They re-mained, neverthelefs, with what Intent God the Lord only knows.

Their Sackimas called before the Council and promife to de-part.

Meanwhile, the honeft Burgh-

2

ers, irritated at the Insults suf-
fered throughout that Day, very
prudently and through fear of
further Mischief, doubled the
Guards during the following
Night, by command of the remaining Councillors and other
Officers.   About eight o'clock,
one *Paulus Leendertsen* was,
according to his Declaration,
threatened with an Axe, and
the late Fiscal *Van Dyck* was
wounded with an Arrow within this City.   Thereupon great
Uproar and Tumult arose;
some of the Burghers got into
Conflict with the *Indians*, and
some, though few, were killed
on both Sides.   Shortly after-

The Guards
doubled.

Mr. Leendert-
sen threatened
and the late
Fiscal wounded.

Consequent
conflict; some
killed.

wards and throughout the whole
of the following Night, thoſe
Indian Tribes laid waſte the Terrible devaſ-
tation of the ſur-
Settlements by a terrible Fire rounding ſettle-
ments.
and Maſſacre to ſuch an extent
that, in three Days, full *Fifty*
Chriſtians were murdered and Numbers murdered and 100
put to Death; over *One Hun-* captivated.
dred, moſtly Women and Children, were captivated, whereof
Sixty to *Seventy* were afterwards
ranſomed at a great Expenſe,
the Balance ſtill remaining in
their Hands; *Twenty-eight*
Bouweries and a number of
Plantations were burnt with full Farms laid
waſte and crops
Twelve to *Fifteen Hundred* deſtroyed.
Skepels of Grain; and *Five* to
Six Hundred head of Cattle

either killed or ftill in poffeffion
of the Barbarians.   Truly,
Right Honorable, Your Subjects
and humble Petitioners have at
the hands of thefe Barbarous
Savages, fuffered a lofs of twice
One Hundred Thoufand Guilders; and over *Three Hundred*
Souls, exclufive of thofe who
have been flain or led away
into Captivity, are difpoffeffed
of their Properties and not left
wherewithall to provide Food
and Raiment either for them-
felves or their Families, have
now become a Burthen to the
Burghers of this City alone.
Finally, the Country in general
is fo impoverifhed that it will

Eftimated lofs.

Impoverifhed
condition of
New Nether-
land.

not for Years be brought back
to the flouriſhing Condition in
which it was *Six* ſhort Weeks
ago.

When to all this is ſuper-
added the Fear which poſſeſſes,
and not without reaſon, the
majority of the Inhabitants of Inhabitants unwilling to re-
being again as ſuddenly ſur- turn to their
Bouweries.
prized, in caſe no Remedy be
employed againſt ſo general a
Maſſacre and ſo vaſt a Loſs, it
cauſes them and many others
to be cautious, and afraid of
again returning to the *Flat-
Land*. Indeed, this is an Im-
poſſibility to them, unleſs others
lend them a helping Hand.
From all which, then, in Con-

clusion, nothing is to be ex-
pected through want of Culti-
vation of the Soil and Failure
of Crops, but Poverty, Want,
Famine, and the final and
utter Ruin of the Country.

Ruin of the
Country immi-
nent.

We, Your Honours' Sub-
jects and humble Petitioners,
lay this sad and sorrowful Condition of ourselves and of the
Country before you, in all
Reverence and Humility, im-
ploring at the same time
Counsel and Assistance how to
act towards those Barbarous
Tribes in return for these and
other Murders, Affronts and
serious Losses. Most unwilling
should we be, without your

Assistance and
advice asked for.

Honours' previous Knowledge,
Counſel and Help, to initiate
an open War, which it is na-
turally impoſſible for us to
wage and bring to a deſirable Unable to wage
war unleſs aid-
Iſſue, unleſs next to God's Aſ- ed.
ſiſtance, we obtain Help and
Aid from our beloved Fatherland.

All which being duly con-
ſidered by us, together with
the preſent Inability of the
Honble Directors of the Incor- Send an agent
to the Weſt In-
porated Weſt India Company dia Company;
to ſend us ſuch and ſo ſpeedy
Succour as the Neceſſity and
Circumſtances of the Country
in general demand, we deem
it expedient, in order to avoid

all Exceptions and Charges of Neglect, in not having given Information to the Supreme Government, to addreſs this our humble Supplication firſt and foremoſt to Your Honours (of the Company) and in addition, but with your previous Knowledge and Approbation, to their High Mightineſſes and the Moſt Worſhipful the Regents of the City Amſterdam, or wherever elſe Your Honours will direct *Cornelis Jacobſen Steenwyck*, our Agent.

To the States General, and to the Burgomaſters of Amſterdam.

The Succour wherewith we hope, with God's merciful Help and Aſſiſtance, to reduce the aforeſaid Barbarous Tribes to

to Obedience, and to poſſeſs the
Land again in Peace and without Fear, ſhould, with Submiſ-
ſion to your Honours' better
Judgment, conſiſt of *Three* or
Four Thouſand (*a*) good Soldiers,
armed one-half with Match-
locks, one-half with Wheel-
locks (*Snaphance*) of *three* and
one-half feet Barrel, carrying
Sixteen Bullets to the Pound
and no more, who after the
Work is done would be willing
to ſettle in the Country for the
increaſe of its Population. A
Supply to the amount of *Thirty*
or *Forty Thouſand* Guilders, in

Number of ſol-
diers required;
their arms.

(*a*) The figures are 3 or 400 in another draft of the petition.

3

fuitable Commodities for the Clothing and Support of the Military, is moſt urgently required, together with fome neceſſary Ammunition according to the annexed Liſt.

Right Honourable Lords and Patroons:

We Your Honours' Subjects and Petitioners humbly fupplicate you to take this our humble Remonſtrance and Supplication into your ferious Confideration, and fo to favor us, that we may fpeedily receive good Advice and Aſſiſtance before greater Mifchiefs overtake your Subjects either here or on the reduced *South River.* Which doing you will obligate us, and all other your Honours' Subjects, to pray conſtantly for your Honours' Proſperity, and to remain, Right Honourable, Prudent and Honourable Lords,

Your Honours'

Humble Servants.

APPENDIX.

Treaty of Sixteen Hundred and Forty-five.

THIS day, the *Thirtieth* of *Auguſt*, 1645, before the Director and Council in preſence of the entire Commonalty, appeared in Fort *Amſterdam* theſe *Sackemakers* or Indian Chiefs, both for themſelves and acting on the behalf of the circumjacent Chiefs, *To-wit:*

Oratany Chief of *Achkinckeſhacky;* *Seſekemus* and *William*, Chiefs of *Tappaen* and *Rechgawawanck; Pacham, Pennekeck*, who were here yeſterday and left Power with the former; reſponding alſo for thoſe of *Onany* and their Neighbours; *Mayauwetinnemin* for thoſe of *Marech-*

kawick, *Nayeck* and their Neighbours; together with *Aepjen*, in perſon, ſpeaking for the *Wappinex*, *Wiquacſkeckx*, *Sint-ſings* and *Kichtawangs;*

I. They agree to and conclude a firm, irrefragable Peace with us, which they have promiſed, and do promiſe to hold faſt and nevermore to break.

II. If it come to paſs, which God forbid, that any Difficulty ſhould ariſe between us and them, no War ſhall be commenced on that Account, but they ſhall apply to our *Governour* and we to their *Sackemakers,* and if any one be killed or murdered, Juſtice ſhall be immediately done to the Murderer, and we ſhall live henceforth in all Friendſhip together.

III. They ſhall not come armed near any Chriſtians' Houſes on this Iſland of *Manhatan,* and we will not approach theirs with Guns, unleſs accompanied by an Indian to give them Warning.

IV. And whereas they have ſtill an Engliſh Maiden with them, whom they have promiſed to convey to the Engliſh at *Stamford;* this they likewiſe promiſe to do, and if ſhe be not conveyed thither, they promiſe to bring her here and we will pay them the Ranſom which the Engliſh have promiſed for her.

All that is above written we promiſe ſhall be ſtrictly obſerved throughout the whole of *New Netherland.*

Thus done in the Fort, under the *Blue Sky,* before the Council of *New Nether-land* and the intire Commonalty thereunto convoked, in Preſence of the Mohawk Ambaſſadors who were invited to attend as Mediators at this Negotiation of Peace, and *Claes Antoniſen* their Inter-preter and Co-Mediator herein. Dated as above. The Original was ſigned with

The mark of SISIADEGO.

The mark of CLAES NOORMAN.

The mark of ORATANIM.

The mark of Auronge.

The mark of Sesekemus.

The mark of William of Tappaen.

William Kieft.

La Montagne.

The mark of Jacob Stoffelsen.

John Onderhil.

Francis Douthey.

Go. Bacxter.

Richard Smith.

Gysbert Opdyc.

The mark of Aepje Sachem of the Mahikanders.

Jan Eversen Bout.

Oloff Stevensen.

Cornelis Vander Hoykens.

The mark of Cornelis Tonissen.

Lower ſtood :

To my knowledge,

(Signed) Cornelis Van Tienhouen,

Secretary.

Dutch Inhabitants of Gravesend to the Director and Council.

Honourable, wife, prudent and difcreet Sirs,
The Director General and
Council of New Netherland,
Health.

Gravefend, Sept. 8, 1655.
Great and Refpectful Lords!

WE hear here dayly ftrange and uncouth Reports from Heem-fted, Newtown and other places, that the Savages intend to root out the Dutch among the Englifh, de-manding from the Englifh at Grave-fend, that they will feparate themfelves from us, to efcape the danger of lofing, with us, their Lives and Property. They read us yefterday evening, when all were under arms, a Letter to the fame purpofe, of which we here include a copy, with many different reports, too long to be in-ferted here, all have a bearing to induce

4

us to depart from here, as was propofed to us by Tilton and the Magiftrate, it being the fafeft way for us, to preferve our Lives and Property to feparate ourfelves from them, and to depart to the Manhattans, by which means the Englifh too might be faved, as they pretended. But if we were unwilling to depart, that then neverthelefs they would leave nothing untried to fave us. A poor Confolation indeed, as it appears to us if the Indians approach in confiderable numbers. It is further faid, that the Indians from the North, and the adjacent places, were making great preparations to execute their projeƈt, fo that they are urgently exhorting us to depart and fave our Lives as fpeedily as it is poffible.

By thefe ftrong perfuafions we are indeed perplexed and confounded, not knowing what to do or to aƈt, to whom to addrefs ourfelves, except to God Almighty and your Honours, who, we are confident, are willing in this dire neceffity to affift us with your Wifdom and Power, for the Water has already nearly reached our Lips. If we leave this fpot, then Long Ifland no longer has Dutch people for inhabitants. Whereupon we prefume, it well deferves the Attention of your Honours to confider what our Situation requires, although we are unable to difcover what to do in this perilous Situation. We are every day on the alert on foot and on horfeback, to obtain one another's opinion from which your Honours may prefume what Fate is threatening us.

Yefterday Tilton and the Sheriff of Newtown arrived here, to-day they return together from here. If your Hon. deemed it advifable to fave us and Long Ifland, a fmall force would be fully adequate to effect this Purpofe. But, if your Honours did prefer to fee our arrival at the Fort, our hands and feet are unable to provide for the fafety of our wives and children, not even to procure them Victuals. In that cafe it would be indifpenfable to fend a well armed Veffel towards Anthony Janfen's, with fuch a quantity of Provifions as may be deemed proper. But we truft our fituation to your Wifdom and Prudence, confident that you will refolve what is beft and defirable, and we expect your Advice and Orders, agreeably to which we fhall regulate our conduct. We are and remain your Honours Subjects,

JACOBUS VAN CORLER.

JAN THOMASSEN.

HUYBERT JANSEN HOOCK.

JACOB HELLEKAS.

LUYCAS VANDER LIPHORST.

BARENT BALTES.

† mark of HENDRICK CORNELISSEN.

( ) mark of JAN JACOBSEN.

C mark of WILLAM WILLEMSEN.

‡ mark of CORNELIS BEECKEMAN.

Mr. Thomas Wheeler to the People of Gravefend, L. I.

Weſt Cheſter, 27 Sept., 1655.

RESPECTED friends—After my refpects prefented unto you. I am fenfible of your feares; and it is not without grounds: I feare to ufe the beſt means, as is in my power. I ſhall not be wanting in mee to you for your prefervation, to fpeake with the Indians; wee know not how, the Bearer thereof can further informe you, but if you fend a meffenger about Saterday with your minde, I thincke our Saggamaker will be hear, but if you do not, my true endeavor ſhall be ufed for your Safetye and and my weake advife to you at prefent, if you intend your prefervation and alſoe the Dutch, that are amongſt, if they meane to fave theyre Lives, there muſt be meanes ufed for them, to retourne to their own contremen for fafe guard; for this I fully underſtand, that the Indians will pick them out of every Engliſh towne upon the Iſland and in New England. It is a trouble to our Saggamackers, that there is ſo many Dutch among you, for feare they ſhould wrong you in killing of them. Soe deſiring the Lord to proteƈt you I reſt

THOS. WHELER.

The Indians intend no wrong to the Engliſh, if they aſſiſt not the Dutch with men or proviſion.

Affidavit as to the Hoſtility of the Indians.

JOSEPH Safford, Thomas Read, reſiding near Meſpath's kill, declare, that they were informed this day by Joſeph Fowler, Goodman Beets, Samuel Tow, and his ſon-in-law William Read, that ſome of the Inhabitants of Gravefend had been at Weſtcheſter, and that there the Sachemakers of the Savages had been at Lieutenant Wheeler, and that they intended to fend to the Englifh Villages on Long Ifland, that thefe fhould deliver in their hands Tomas Nuton and Harry Nuton and Edward Jefop, becaufe they in that night, when the Savages committed fo much mifchief, affifted the Dutch in the Fort. Further, that the Savages prohibited the Englifh to bring any provifions whatever to the Manhattans, or any fire wood, or affift them with any fort of victuals; and in cafe the Englifh affifted the Dutch with fire wood or any kind of victuals, that then they would burn their hamlets and houfes. They declared that this was true, and were willing to confirm it with their oath.

JOSEPH SAFFORD.

The mark of THOMAS READ.

Lower ftood:

This was written in the prefence of the Hon. La Montagne, and the Hon. Burgomafter Allard Antony, in whofe prefence the witneſſes took their oaths in the hands of the Attorney General.

> · La Montagne.
> Allard Athony.

8 *September,* 1655.

Opinion of Director Stuyveſant.

WE concur in the general Opinion that the Indians had, on their firſt Arrival, no other intention than to wage War againſt the Savages on the eaſt End of Long Iſland. We have come to this Concluſion from various Reaſons too long to be detailed here; and that a culpable want of Vigilance, and a too haſty Raſhneſs on the part of a few hot-headed Spirits, had diverted the Indians and been the cauſe of the dreadful Conſequences and enormous Loſſes.

Opinion of Councillor La Montagne.

...... IT muſt be firſt aſcertained whe-
ther the Indians were the firſt
Aggreſſors or not. This muſt
be determined from their previous Action,
for granting that they did not intend any
Harm in their Proceeding, yet having
excited a reaſonable Suſpicion, and occa-
ſioned this Conflict, they will always be
deemed the Inſtigators and Aggreſſors,
and therefore the *Cauſa movens* thereof.

And *firſt:* Was not their unſeaſonable,
unannounced and unauthorized collecting
here of *Nineteen hundred* Savages, *Eight
hundred* of whom had already landed, to
make an attack on *Fifty* or *Sixty*, contrary to their uſual Cuſtoms, ſufficient to
create a Suſpicion of an evil Intent? and
did not the intollerable Inſolencies which
they committed in breaking into Mr.
Allerton's Houſe, and beating ſome Burghers in their own Houſes, increaſe that

Sufpicion afterwards? Did not their remaining here, contrary to their Promife, and the Murder which they fought to commit, after the fetting of the Watch, on Captain *Paulus Leendertfen*, afford fufficient Grounds for concluding an evil Intention on their part? And were not all the Burghers, who were to be muftered in the Fort for its Security, and being there (fince they were not called out to guard the Fort only but to protect the intire Place), were they not in duty bound to fuccour any Burgher who cried out, *Murder! Help!* And coming there, and finding the Burgher wounded in the Breaft by an Arrow, were they not bound to run to the Indians for the purpofe of examining their Faces, and when they found them with Arms and Guns, were they not juftified in making a ftand againft them? . . . . . .

Before the Attack, they had murdered, in the North, *Ten* of our People at dif-

ferent Times, contrary to the Peace con-
cluded between them and us, without
manifefting the leaft Willingnefs to make
us any Reparation. After the Attack, they
flaughtered ever fo many People, Men,
Women and Children; took numbers of
Prifoners; burned many Bouweries and
Plantations, and deftroyed a Quantity of
Cattle, in violation of the Article of the
Peace fpecially fought for by them,
which provided—*That in cafe any of our
People or theirs happened to be killed, no
War fhall be waged on that account againft
each other, before and until Reparation and
Accommodation had been applied for, and
refufed.* . . . . .

Thofe of *Ahafiemes, Hachkinkefhacky,
Tappan* and others were alfo in this
Attack. They did our People the moft
Damage and wrought the moft cruel
Barbarity by murdering *Seven* Men and
One Woman, whom they flaughtered in
cold Blood, in violation of their Promife

confirmed by an Oath, never taken before by them, To-wit : *May God who is above wreak Vengeance on us if we do not keep our Promiſe.*

Opinion of Fiſcal Van Tienhoven.

PEACE having been concluded with the Natives in Auguſt *Sixteen Hundred five* and *forty*, both it and its Proviſions have been infringed and broken by the Indians, as follow :

I.

By the Murder of *Fourteen* Chriſtians in divers Places and at divers Times, between Auguſt *Sixteen Hundred five* and *forty* and the *fifteenth* of September, *Sixteen Hundred five* and *fifty*. Although demanded according to the Treaty, we have never been able to obtain Juſtice much leſs Satisfaction therefor, but on the contrary, they have paid us with Lies and falſe Reports, as the *Honourable* the Director-General, the Council, the Inhabitants of this Country, and our Neighbours well know.

II.

On the *Seventeenth* of laſt September, did the Indians violate and break the Treaty of Peace by force in this City of *Amſterdam*, in manner as followeth:

Firſt. Very early in the Morning, without having given any previous notice, they landed on the Shore within the Walls of this City, with *Sixty-four* Canoes and about *Five hundred* Men, all armed; and immediately after their arrival, before ſcarcely any Burghers were afoot, a large Troop of them, in Arms, ruſhed through the Streets, and forcibly breaking open Mr. *Allerton's* Houſe, knocking the Lock off the Door, and beating the Inmates, ſearched the Premiſes by main Force, under Pretence of looking for Northern Indians. They acted in like Manner, alſo, in many Houſes within this City, until, on the Complaint of the Inhabitants and in order to prevent Mifchief, they were fhown from the *Heere Straete* (*a*) to the Shore of the *North River*, where their Canoes lay, and they had difembarked in the Morning.

The Chiefs or *Sackimaas* of the Indians, confifting of divers Nations, were invited in a friendly Manner to appear at the Council Chamber in the Fort. They did fo, and were there afked by the Members of the Council then attending, in the Prefence of the Burgomafters, Schepens and the Burgher Military Officers, the Reafon for their coming fo armed and without having given previous Notice; alfo, why they and their People committed fuch Violence and Outrage on the Burghers, breaking Locks, knocking at Doors, pufhing People and fearching Houfes, which no Dutchman could do without the Order and Authority of

(*a*) Broadway.

the Government. Therefore, the Councillors prefent and the aforefaid Burgher
Officers requefted that the Indians, for
their and our greater Security and to
prevent Mifchief and Misfortune, would
depart before Sun-down from this Ifland
to the *Nut Ifland.* This they promifed
to do, whereupon they then took their
Departure.

In ftead of keeping their Promife to
depart, there came to them in the Evening *Two Hundred* armed Indians, who,
after the fetting of the Watch, fhot
Hendrick Van Dyck, late Fifcal, with an
Arrow in his Breaft, and threatened to
fhoot *Paulus Leendertfen*, Burgher-Cap-
tain, with an Arrow. Upon thefe and
other Occurrences, the Cry arofe—
*Murder! Murder! the Indians are mur-
dering the Dutch!* Whereupon the
Burghers ftationed in the Fort under
Arms in order to keep good Watch, ran,
on a further Outcry, in Confufion and

without any Orders, fome through the Gate, others over the Walls, fo that they came into Conflict with the Indians who were lying ready about the Shore. *Two* Dutchmen lay killed, and *three* wounded on the Strand, and *three* Indians were found dead.

This Rencountre having fo come to pafs, the Indians taking their Courfe acrofs the River and elfewhere, burnt many Houfes, murdered and captivated Chriftians, killed Cattle, and after a lapfe of fome Days ftripped *Staten Ifland* of People and Houfes, which alfo, is in violation of the Articles of the Peace concluded Anno *Sixteen Hundred five* and *forty,* whereby it was expreffly contracted, *That in cafe one or more Perfons were killed or murdered, no General War fhall immediately follow, but the injured Party fhall complain to the Chiefs or Rulers of thofe who commit the Deed, in order that Juftice be done to the Malefactors according to Circumftances.*

*Lift of Yeomanry, Men, Women and Chil-
dren, Men and Maid Servants, fent by
Baron Hendrick van de Capelle tot
Ryffel to New Netherland, in the Weft
Indies, on Staten Ifland, fince May,
1650, and who furvived that cruel and
bloody Deftruction by the Indians, in
September, 1655.*

1. Capt. Andriaen Pos, with wife, five
children, one fervant, one girl; refide yet
on the Ifland.

2. Hendrik Werrinck, with wife, two
children, and one fervant; refide on Manhattans.

3. Paul Derricks, wife, one child, and
one fervant; refide at Fort Orange.

4. Hendrik Marcellis, wife, two children, one fervant; refide at Fort Orange.

5. Jan Aertfen van Heerde, with wife
and eight children, refide at Manhattans.

6. Albert Gyfbertfen van Heerde, wife,

four children, one fervant; refide at Fort Orange.

7. The wife of Arent van Hengel was married with one Severyn, now living at Manhattans. This woman hath a fon.

8. The widow of John van Oldenfeel, named Elfken, married one Mandemaker, with three children; lives on Long Ifland.

9. The widow of Jan Weffelinck, married to an Englifhman, being a carman living at the Manhattans, with three children.

10. Dylart, fervant of the deceafed farmer, refides at Mefpathfkill.

11. The wife of a Wheelwright, who was engaged at Zutphen, named Herminken, refides at Fort Orange, and married a Carpenter with two children.

12. Three children of corporal Gerrit Janffen van Steenwyck, tranfported hither at the Baron's expenfe.

13. Wynold, fervant of deceafed Hans Barentfen van Ofnabrugge, fent by Melyn

towards the north, has left him again, and has become an apprentice to a ſhip carpenter.

14. A boy of Barent Drieſſen van Ooſteveng, lives with a farmer on Long Iſland.

15. A child from Heenderen, called " the maimed child," reſides at Breukelen, oppoſite Manhattans.

In all 67 living ſouls. Recorded in this manner at Zutphen, on the 14th November, 1657, by the wife of Capt. Pos, and by the farmer Jan Aertſen van Heerde.

Proclamation.

Honourable, Beloved, Faithful!

IT cannot, at leaſt ought not, be unknown to, or forgotten by, any among us, that the all good and gracious God hath vouchſafed to, and beſtowed upon, this budding Province and the Inhabitants thereof, many ſpecial

Favours, Bleffings and Benefits, among the leaft of which are an increafe of Population; a Merciful Protection againft a menacing and dreaded War with our Neighbours, unexpectedly transformed into a wifhed-for and acceptable Peace; a particular augmentation of Profperity and Trade, and a bountiful and blefled Harveft and continued Health.

As we ufed not with fufficient care, but rather ungratefully abufed thefe Favours and many other of God's Special Benefits and Bleffings, God hath been moved for our Admonition, to change his Favours towards us, vifiting and juftly chaftening, if not punifhing, us at the going out of the laft Year, by a fudden and unexpected Incurfion of the Wild Barbarous Natives of thefe Lands, by whofe cruel and murderous Hands many Inhabitants of this Province were pitilefsly murdered and bereft of Property and Life; many Bouweries, Plantations and Houfes burned, and the common Weal fo thrown back, that we may with juftice exclaim with the Prophet in the *Lamentations :* How hath the Lord covered us with a Cloud in his Anger and caft down from Heaven unto the Earth the beauty of the Land : The Lord hath fwallowed up our Habitations and hath not pitied ; He hath cut off in His fierce Anger our Horn ; He hath drawn back His right Hand from before the Enemy, and He burnt as a raging Fire, which devoureth all around us, who ftill are fpared like a Hovel in a Cucumber Garden, as a warning that all of us fhall in like Manner perifh, unlefs we turn us from our Ingratitude and heinous Sins ; we who ftill remain being Sinners no lefs than the other Inhabitants of this Province on whom we have feen fall not the Tower of Siloh but the Wrath of God out of the Heavens, which through want of Care and true Penance is ftill hanging over our Heads.

In order then to deprecate this from the All good God, and to draw again on us, in place of His righteous Punifhment, His gracious Favours, Bleffings and Benefits, We the Director General and Council of *New Netherland,* have deemed it highly neceffary to ordain a Day of General Fafting and Prayer, which fhall be holden on the firft *Wednefday* in the Month of *March,* being the *firft* day of the faid Month; therefore we charge all our Subjects to repair in the fore and after Noon of the Day aforefaid, to the Church, or where Men are wont to hear God's Word, in order, after hearing the fame, with contrite and humble Hearts, to invoke together, with one Accord, the Name of the Lord; to Pray and Implore His Divine Majefty to be pleafed to ftay the Flood of His Wrath and the Clouds of His Anger, which began to pour down on us, and to change them into Streams of his ancient Favour and Mercy, avert-

ing all deftroying War from us and all
our good Inhabitants, or fhould His Majefty otherwife order, for the Glory of
His Name, the wider Propagation of His
Gofpel and for the Security of this Province and its Inhabitants, then that the
all Beneficent God would pleafe our
flender Might and Mean fo to blefs; to
endue the Director General and Council
together with all Inferiour Officers, People
and Subjects with Wifdom, Underftand-
ing and Fortitude, to the End that the
good Inhabitants, brought hither by his
Hand and outftretched Arm, and hitherto
protected againft the Power and Cruelty
of a Barbarous People, may be taken and
remain henceforth fheltered under His
Wings, and that fuch Means may to that
End be defigned and put in practice as
His Majefty will vouchfafe to blefs to the
greater Glory of His Name. Likewife
to pray God the Lord for continuous
Health and Profperity of Trade and

Agriculture, but chiefly for a proper and grateful Ufe of his gracious Favours and Benefits.

To the End that all this may be better, more zealoufly and more unanimoufly put in Practice, we interdict and forbid, during Divine Service, on the aforefaid Day of Fasting and Prayer, all playing of Ball and Billiards, all Hunting, Fifhing, Sailing, Plowing, Sowing, Mowing, and all unlawful Games, fuch as Dice and Intemperance, under pain of Arbitrary Correction and Punifhment, hereunto provided. In like Manner, will we have all Minifters of God's Holy Word, within our Government, admonifhed and requefted to adapt their Sermons and Prayers to the End aforefaid. Thus done and concluded in our Council holden in Fort *Amfterdam* in *New Netherland* the *twentyfeventh* January, Anno 1656.